Retire Rich with a Salary Sacrifice Pension

How to Boost Your Pension Pot by over £50,000 at the Taxman's Expense

By Nick Braun PhD

Important Legal Notices:

Taxcafe®
Tax Guide - "Retire Rich with a Salary Sacrifice Pension"

Published by:
Taxcafe UK Limited
67 Milton Road
Kirkcaldy KY1 1TL
Tel: (0044) 01592 560081
Email: team@taxcafe.co.uk

Second edition, April 2011

ISBN 978-1-907302-35-0

Disclaimer
Before reading or relying on the content of this tax guide please read the disclaimer carefully. If you have any queries then please contact the publisher at team@taxcafe.co.uk.

Need Affordable & Expert Tax Planning Help?

Try Taxcafe's Unique Question & Answer Service

The purpose of Taxcafe guides is to provide you with detailed guidance, giving you all the information you need to make informed decisions.

Ultimately, you may want to take further action or obtain guidance personal to your circumstances.

Taxcafe.co.uk has a unique online tax help service that provides access to highly qualified tax professionals at an affordable rate.

For more information or to take advantage of this service please visit:

www.taxcafe.co.uk/questions

Disclaimer

1. Please note that this publication is intended as **general guidance only** and does NOT constitute accountancy, tax, financial or other professional advice. The author and Taxcafe UK Limited make no representations or warranties with respect to the accuracy or completeness of the contents of this publication and cannot accept any responsibility for any liability, loss or risk, personal or otherwise, which may arise, directly or indirectly, from reliance on information contained in this publication.

2. Please note that tax legislation, the law and practices of government and regulatory authorities (e.g. Revenue & Customs) are constantly changing. Furthermore, your personal circumstances may vary from the general information contained in this guide which may not be suitable for your situation. We therefore recommend that for accountancy, tax, financial or other professional advice, you consult a suitably qualified accountant, tax specialist, independent financial adviser, or other professional adviser. Your professional adviser will be able to provide specific advice based on your personal circumstances.

3. This book covers taxation applying to UK residents only. Please note that references to the 'UK' do not include the Channel Islands or the Isle of Man. The tax position of non-UK residents is beyond the scope of this book.

4. All persons described in the examples in this book are entirely fictional characters created specifically for the purposes of this guide. Any similarities to actual persons, living or dead, or to fictional characters created by any other author, are entirely coincidental.

Dedication

Once again, to Aileen for all your love and support and to Jake, Sandy and Tilly for all the joy you bring.

About the Author & Taxcafe

Nick Braun founded Taxcafe in Edinburgh in 1999 along with his partner, Aileen Smith. As the driving force behind the company, their aim is to provide affordable plain-English tax information for private individuals and investors, business owners, IFAs and accountants.

Since then Taxcafe has become one of the best-known tax publishers in the UK and won several business awards.

Nick has been involved in the tax publishing world since 1989 as a writer, editor and publisher. He holds a masters degree and PhD in economics from the University of Glasgow, where he was awarded the prestigious William Glen Scholarship and later became a Research Fellow.

Prior to that he graduated with distinction from the University of South Africa, the country's oldest university, earning the highest economics results in the university's history. He went on to become editor of *Personal Finance* and *Tax Breaks*, two of South Africa's best-known financial publications, before moving to the UK in 1994.

Nick is also an Enrolled Agent, a tax professional recognized by the United States federal government to represent taxpayers in dealings with the Internal Revenue Service (IRS).

When he's not working, Nick likes to spend time with his children and eat good food!

Contents

Introduction

How would you like to increase your pension pot by up to 34%, with the taxman footing the entire bill?

It seems too good to be true but this result can be achieved if you stop making pension contributions *personally* and get your employer to make them for you.

This set-up is known as salary sacrifice and it is used by some of the country's biggest companies, universities and other organisations, including BT, Tesco and the BBC. Most important of all, salary sacrifice has the taxman's full blessing!

So how does it work? Salary sacrifice is all about saving *national insurance*, on top of the income tax relief you already receive when you make pension contributions. Saving national insurance has become more important than ever, following the one percentage point increase in rates that took effect on 6th April 2011.

Most people only enjoy income tax relief when they contribute to a pension: Basic-rate taxpayers save 20% tax and higher-rate taxpayers normally save 40% tax. So a £1,000 pension contribution made by a higher-rate taxpayer will normally result in a tax saving of £400.

The income tax relief on pension contributions is attractive but it's not the maximum amount of tax relief available. When an individual contributes personally to a pension plan there is no refund of all the national insurance paid by both the employee and the employer.

Since 6th April 2011, as much as £258 of national insurance is paid by the employee and employer on £1,000 of salary.

With salary sacrifice arrangements, it is possible to put a stop to these national insurance payments because your employer makes your pension contributions for you.

Pension contributions paid by employers are exempt from national insurance.

The national insurance savings can then be added to your pension pot.

Sacrificing Salary, Not Income

Because the employer has to pay the employee's pension contributions, the employee in return has to sacrifice some salary.

However, it's important to stress that the employee's **disposable income** will not fall – it remains exactly the same.

Salary sacrifice arrangements can also be structured so that take home pay goes up, with pensions contributions remaining the same.

In fact, with salary sacrifice there are no losers: Both the employee and employer can save money. The only loser is the taxman!

Company Pension Scheme Not Required

Salary sacrifice can be used by individual employees or groups of employees – it doesn't have to be available en masse.

Furthermore, it is not necessary to belong to some sort of company pension scheme. Salary sacrifice works with almost all pension plans including:

- Self-invested personal pensions (SIPPs)
- Personal pensions (group and individual plans)
- Stakeholder pensions (group and individual plans)
- Occupational pension schemes

The main consideration is that the plan must be able to accept employer contributions. Many SIPP providers have special forms for this purpose.

Final Salary Schemes

Salary sacrifice is mostly about making bigger pension contributions at the taxman's expense.

However, employees who belong to final salary pension schemes do not care about making bigger pension contributions because their pensions depend on how many years they've been employed and how much they earn. The contributions are generally the employer's problem.

However, members of final salary pension schemes can enjoy an increase in their take-home pay if they belong to a salary sacrifice pension scheme. Those who stand to benefit most are basic-rate taxpayers.

Tax and Pension Basics

Before we look at some examples of how salary sacrifice works in practice, I'm going to step back very briefly and cover some basics including:

- How income tax and national insurance is calculated
- How tax relief on pension contributions is calculated
- Some important new pension plan rules

These three chapters are very short and, after reading them, you will be better equipped to follow the examples in the rest of this guide.

Scope of this Guide

Salary sacrifice can be used by most employees. However, sole traders and other self-employed individuals cannot use salary sacrifice because there is no employer to make pension contributions on their behalf.

There has to be an employer/employee relationship for a salary sacrifice arrangement to be successful.

Finally, please remember that this guide is not meant to substitute for proper professional advice. Before you act you should contact either a suitably qualified accountant, tax advisor, IFA or pensions expert who understands your personal circumstances.

Chapter 1

Income Tax & National Insurance: A Five Minute Primer!

There are lots of examples in this guide and many of them use income tax and national insurance rates and allowances.

In this chapter I'm going to briefly explain how income tax and national insurance is calculated for the average salary earning employee.

This should make the examples easier to understand (and slightly less painful!)

Calculating Income Tax

For the 2011/12 tax year, starting on 6th April 2011, most employees pay income tax as follows:

- 0%   on the first   £7,475   (personal allowance)
- 20%   on the next   £35,000   (basic-rate band)
- 40%   above   £42,475   (higher-rate threshold)

Generally speaking, if you earn more than £42,475 you are a higher-rate taxpayer; if you earn less you are a basic-rate taxpayer.

Example – Basic-Rate Taxpayer

John earns a salary of £30,000. His income tax for 2011/12 can be calculated as follows:

- *0%   on the first   £7,475   =   £0*
- *20%   on the next   £22,525   =   £4,505*

Total income tax bill: £4,505

Example – Higher-Rate Taxpayer

Jane earns a salary of £60,000. Her income tax for 2011/12 can be calculated as follows:

- *0%*   *on the first*   *£7,475*   =   *£0*
- *20%*   *on the next*   *£35,000*   =   *£7,000*
- *40%*   *on the final*   *£17,525*   =   *£7,010*

Total income tax bill: £14,010

Income above £100,000 and £150,000

When your income exceeds £100,000 your tax-free personal allowance is withdrawn and when your income exceeds £150,000 you also start paying tax at 50%. High income earners are covered in Chapter 7.

Calculating National Insurance

Saving national insurance has become more and more important in recent years because the Government has continually widened the net and increased the rates.

For the current 2011/12 tax year employees pay national insurance as follows:

- 0%   on the first   £7,225   (earnings threshold)
- 12%   on the next   £35,250
- 2%   above   £42,475   (upper earnings limit)

Employers pay 13.8% national insurance on every single pound the employee earns over the £7,075 earnings threshold. There is no cap.

You probably don't lose much sleep over your employer's national insurance bill. However, employer's national insurance is a tax on YOUR income. If it didn't exist your employer would be able to pay you a higher salary.

As we will see shortly, salary sacrifice pension arrangements involve taking employer's national insurance away from the taxman and sticking it in your pension pot!

Here are John and Jane's national insurance calculations:

Example – Basic-Rate Taxpayer

John earns a salary of £30,000. His national insurance for 2011/12 can be calculated as follows:

- *0%   on the first   £7,225   =   £0*
- *12%   on the next   £22,775 = £2,733*

John's national insurance bill: £2,733

John's employer pays national insurance on John's salary as follows:

- *0%   on the first   £7,075   =   £0*
- *13.8% on the next   £22,925 = £3,164*

John's employer's national insurance bill: £3,164

Example – Higher-Rate Taxpayer

Jane earns a salary of £60,000. Her national insurance for 2011/12 can be calculated as follows:

- *0%   on the first   £7,225   =   £0*
- *12%   on the next   £35,250 = £4,230*
- *2%   on the final   £17,525 = £350*

Jane's national insurance bill: £4,580

Her employer's national insurance is:

- *0%   on the first   £7,075   =   £0*
- *13.8% on the next   £52,925 = £7,304*

Jane's employer's national insurance bill: £7,304

Tax Bills Combined

John's and Jane's tax bills can be summarised as follows:

John – Basic-rate Taxpayer – £30,000

	£
Income tax	4,505
Employee's national insurance	2,733
Employer's national insurance	3,164
Total taxes	**10,402**

Jane – Higher-rate Taxpayer – £60,000

	£
Income tax	14,010
Employee's national insurance	4,580
Employer's national insurance	7,304
Total taxes	**25,894**

When you include employer's national insurance it's startling how much tax is paid even by those on relatively modest incomes. Direct taxes on John's income come to 35%.

Jane's £60,000 salary is not low by any standards but you wouldn't describe her as a high income earner either. Nevertheless an amount equivalent to 43% of her salary is paid in direct taxes on her income.

Of course, both are also subject to a raft of indirect taxes, based on how they spend what's left, including VAT, council tax, fuel and car taxes, alcohol and tobacco taxes, stamp duty, air passenger duty, *etc.*

Chapter 2

Pension Tax Relief: How You Calculate It

When you contribute to a pension plan you normally enjoy income tax relief.

With company pension schemes your pension contributions are normally deducted from your gross pay – before tax – which gives you full and immediate tax relief for your contributions.

With personal pensions (including SIPPs) and stakeholder pensions your pension contributions are usually paid out of your net after-tax pay. This means all of your tax relief has to be recovered. This chapter explains how this happens.

There are two types of pension tax relief: basic-rate tax relief (claiming back the first 20% tax you pay) and higher-rate relief (claiming back the second 20% tax).

Basic-Rate Relief

Basic-rate tax relief is claimed on your behalf by the company that manages your pension plan (the likes of Hargreaves Lansdown, Standard Life etc). The money is added to your pension pot.

For every £80 you personally invest in your pension plan, the taxman will put in an extra £20, effectively refunding the 20% tax you have already paid. So whatever contribution you make personally, divide it by 0.8 and you will get the total amount that is invested in your plan.

Example

John invests £1,000 in a personal pension. The total amount that will be invested, after the taxman's top-up payment is added, is:

$$£1,000/0.80 = £1,250$$

Higher Rate Relief – The Cherry on Top

If you are a higher-rate taxpayer (generally someone who earns more than £42,475 this year) you can claim the extra 20% tax relief when you submit your tax return.

To calculate your higher-rate tax relief you generally just multiply your gross pension contribution by 20%.

Your gross pension contribution is your personal contribution plus the taxman's top up – i.e. the amount that ends up inside your pension plan.

Example

*Jane earns £60,000 and is a higher-rate taxpayer. She personally contributes £2,400 to her pension plan. Her total **gross** pension contribution, including the taxman's top up, is:*

$$£2,400/0.80 = £3,000$$

Multiplying her gross contribution by 20% we obtain her higher-rate income tax relief:

$$£3,000 \times 20\% = £600$$

This is the amount of income tax that will be refunded to Jane.

Effectively Jane has a pension investment of £3,000 which has cost her just £1,800 (£2,400 personal contribution less her £600 tax refund).

In effect, she is getting all of her pension investments at a 40% discount.

Shortcut Calculation

A quicker way to calculate Jane's tax refund is to multiply the amount she personally contributes by 25%.

Example Revisited

Jane is a higher-rate taxpayer and personally contributes £2,400 to her pension plan.

Her tax refund is:

$$£2,400 \times 25\% = £600$$

Limits to Higher-Rate Tax Relief

If you are a higher-rate taxpayer you will only receive higher-rate tax relief on your entire pension contribution if you have sufficient earnings taxed at 40%.

Example

Helga earns a salary of £48,000 and makes a pension contribution of £8,640. Including the taxman's top up, her total gross pension contribution is £10,800.

However, only £5,525 of Helga's earnings are subject to 40% higher-rate tax (£48,000 - £42,475).

This means she cannot claim the maximum £2,160 of higher-rate tax relief on the pension contribution (£10,800 x 20%).

Instead she is entitled to higher-rate tax relief of just £1,105 (£5,525 x 20%.

In all of the examples in this guide, unless otherwise stated, it is assumed that higher-rate taxpayers receive the maximum tax relief on their pension contributions.

Changes to Pension Tax Relief

The previous Labour Government decided that anyone earning over £150,000 would have their higher-rate tax relief withdrawn, starting in April 2011. Tax relief would only be available at the basic rate once your income reached £180,000.

After the general election in June 2010 there were also fears that the new coalition Government would go one step further and scrap higher-rate tax relief for EVERYBODY. This, after all, was a Liberal Democrat election pledge, made in the interests of 'fairness'.

In October 2010, after spending several months consulting industry experts, the Government released its proposals to change tax relief on pension contributions.

Fortunately, the news was very good. Most readers will find that they can save as much as they like in a pension plan and continue enjoying the maximum tax relief.

Both the Labour and Liberal Democrat proposals have been confined to the dustbin. Higher-rate tax relief has not been taken away from anyone.

Those who earn over £150,000 have had their full higher-rate tax relief restored. In fact, it gets better than this. Because these individuals pay 50% income tax, they now enjoy 50% tax relief on their pension contributions.

We know this because the Government announced that tax relief will be available at your marginal tax rate (i.e. 20%, 40% or 50%).

So what's the catch?

The Government has decided to limit the amount that you can invest each year into your pension plan. Fortunately, most taxpayers will find the new contribution limits very generous.

The maximum pension contribution you can make – the so-called 'annual allowance' – has been reduced from £255,000 to £50,000 with effect from 6th April 2011.

£50,000 is the maximum *gross* contribution you can make and includes the taxman's 20% top up. The maximum *cash* contribution you can make is £40,000.

Making Bigger Pension Contributions

The new rules contain some extra flexibility.

If you want to contribute more than £50,000 during any given tax year, you will be able to tap any unused allowance from the three previous tax years. So you could potentially make a pension contribution of up to almost £200,000 and enjoy full tax relief.

The Lifetime Allowance

Starting in the 2012/13 tax year the so-called 'lifetime allowance' – the maximum pension pot you can build up during your lifetime – will be reduced from £1.8 million to £1.5 million.

Summary

- When you make personal pension contributions you generally qualify for two different types of tax relief: Basic-rate income tax relief which comes in the shape of top-ups to your pension plan and higher-rate relief which takes the shape of an income tax refund paid to you personally.

- Your total gross pension contribution (the amount that ends up in your pension plan) is found by dividing your personal contribution by 0.80. The extra money is paid into your pension pot by the taxman.

- Higher-rate relief (your income tax refund) is calculated by multiplying your gross pension fund contribution by 20%.

- Alternatively, you can calculate your higher-rate relief by multiplying the amount you personally contribute by 25%.

- Together these two tax reliefs mean all your pension investments come in at a 40% discount, if you are a higher-rate taxpayer.

- The pension contribution rules have changed, with effect from 6th April 2011.

- The maximum gross contribution now is £50,000 per year but everyone will enjoy tax relief at their marginal income tax rate: 20%, 40% or even 50%.

Chapter 3

Pension Plan Basics

The rules governing the various types of pension scheme are quite complex. However, just as you don't need to know anything about engines to drive a car, you can contribute to a pension plan and save tax without knowing all the ins and outs.

Key points worth knowing are the following:

- Anyone under 75 years of age can make pension contributions.

- Pension contributions normally enjoy income tax relief – for every £1 you contribute, £1 of your earnings will be effectively tax free.

- Pension contributions normally do not enjoy national insurance relief – one exception is contributions paid by employers. That's what this guide is all about!

- The new maximum pension contribution is £50,000 per tax year and you can tap any unused allowance from the three previous tax years.

- The maximum pension contribution you can make is restricted to the amount of your earnings (e.g. if your earnings are £20,000 your maximum contribution is £20,000).

- 'Earnings' include salary or profits from a sole trader business. Earnings do not include dividends, interest and rental profits.

- Everyone under age 75 can make a pension contribution of up to £3,600 and enjoy tax relief, even those with no earnings (e.g. minor children and those who do not work).

- You can have more than one pension plan. For example, if you belong to an employer's occupational pension scheme you can also contribute privately to a self-invested personal pension (SIPP).

- The investments you make with your pension contributions grow free of income tax and capital gains tax.

- When you reach age 55 you can start withdrawing money from any personal pension plan.

- You can withdraw 25% of your pension savings as a tax-free lump sum.

- The remaining 75% is generally withdrawn gradually as income which is fully taxed.

Chapter 4

Salary Sacrifice Case Study: Basic-Rate Taxpayer

Introduction

In this chapter we are going to follow the same John from Chapters 1 and 2 and show how he can increase his total pension pot by 34% with a salary sacrifice arrangement.

Remember John earns £30,000 and is a basic-rate taxpayer (a basic-rate taxpayer is generally someone earning less than £42,475). Basic-rate taxpayers pay 20% income tax and 12% national insurance.

We will look at how higher-rate taxpayers can benefit from salary sacrifice in the next chapter.

John's Retirement Savings

We know from Chapter 1 that John pays income tax of £4,505 and national insurance of £2,733 on his £30,000 salary.

Let's say he also saves £1,000 (just over 3% of his salary).

After deducting his taxes and savings he is left with a disposable income of £21,762.

John faces a dilemma. He knows he's not saving much but he also has children to support and feels he cannot live on a penny less than £21,762.

On the advice of a friend, John opens a self-invested personal pension (SIPP). He contributes £1,000 and the taxman tops this up with an extra £250 of free cash (basic-rate tax relief), bringing John's total pension saving to £1,250.

In summary, John's pension saving is £1,250 per year, even though his personal contribution is only £1,000. The amount he saves has increased by 25%.

Avoiding National Insurance

This is not a bad outcome but John can do much better.

So far he has enjoyed full *income tax* relief on his pension contributions. However, income tax is not the only tax John pays. He also pays 12% national insurance on most of his salary and his employer pays 13.8%.

Unfortunately, there is no national insurance relief for pension contributions made directly by employees like John. In other words, when he contributes to his SIPP he receives back all of the income tax he has paid on the amount contributed but none of the national insurance.

However, there is full national insurance relief for pension contributions made by employers.

John therefore decides to stop contributing personally to his pension and asks his employer to make the contributions for him. In return, John agrees to sacrifice some salary.

John's Salary Sacrifice

John sacrifices £1,471 which takes his salary from £30,000 to £28,529 (we will explain why he sacrifices this exact amount in Chapter 6).

After deducting income tax and national insurance on £28,529 he is still left with £21,762 – the exact amount of income we know he needs to live on.

John's employer pays the £1,471 of sacrificed salary directly into John's pension plan. His employer also contributes an additional £203, representing the employer's national insurance saving:

$$£1,471 \times 13.8\% = £203$$

Remember, employers pay national insurance on salaries but not on pension contributions.

The amount going into John's pension pot now is £1,674.

In summary, John still has £21,762 of take-home pay, just as before, but his pension contribution has increased from £1,250 to £1,674 – an increase of 34%.

Remember, before John started contributing to a pension plan he was not enjoying any national insurance relief OR income tax relief and was saving just £1,000 per year.

Now he is enjoying full income tax and national insurance relief and the amount he saves has increased by 67%.

In summary, John is avoiding 20% income tax, 12% employee's national insurance and 13.8% employer's national insurance on the money he contributes to his pension plan.

A summary of the number crunching can be found on the next page.

John's Take Home Pay Stays the Same

	Before Salary Sacrifice	After Salary Sacrifice
	£	£
Salary	30,000	28,529
Less:		
Income tax	4,505	4,211
National insurance	2,733	2,556
Pension contribution	1,000	0
Disposable income	**21,762**	**21,762**

... But His Pension Pot Increases By 34%

	Before Salary Sacrifice	After Salary Sacrifice
	£	£
Employee contribution	1,000	-
Taxman's top up	250	-
Employer contribution	-	1,471
Employer's NI saving	-	203
Total	**1,250**	**1,674**

Long-Term Picture

So far we have taken a one-year snapshot. Pension plans are long-term savings vehicles, so it's important to examine how salary sacrifice affects John's pension pot over a period of, say, 10 years.

The table below shows how John's pension pot grows with and without salary sacrifice.

Year	Without Sacrifice £	With Sacrifice £
1	1,250	1,674
2	2,588	3,465
3	4,019	5,382
4	5,550	7,432
5	7,188	9,627
6	8,942	11,975
7	10,818	14,487
8	12,825	17,175
9	14,972	20,051
10	17,271	23,129

There are a couple of assumptions behind these numbers:

- **John's annual pension contribution is the same every year.** This assumption keeps things simple but does not affect what the example seeks to illustrate. So John's pension contribution every year is £1,250 (without salary sacrifice) and £1,674 (with salary sacrifice).

- **John's investments grow by 7% per year tax free.** This assumption also does not affect what the example is trying to illustrate.

To explain how each number in the table is calculated let's look at John's position without salary sacrifice and step forward to year two. The number in the table is £2,588. This is made up of his contribution in year one, plus 7% growth on that contribution, plus his contribution in year two:

$$£1,250 + £88 + £1,250 = £2,588$$

Similarly, let's pluck a figure out of the second column, say £11,975 in year six. This consists of the value of John's pension pot in the previous year (£9,627), plus 7% growth on £9,627 (£674), plus his contribution in year six:

$$£9,627 + £674 + £1,674 = £11,975$$

In year 10 John will have £17,271 in his pension pot without salary sacrifice, compared with £23,129 with salary sacrifice. Clearly, salary sacrifice will leave him significantly better off.

The pound amounts, however, are largely meaningless to anyone except John. Your own pension contributions will be either bigger or smaller than his, your investments will probably grow at a different rate and you may be interested in a period lasting longer or shorter than 10 years.

However, what IS relevant is the *percentage difference* between the two columns in the table. Every year it is exactly the same: 34%!

This implies the following for basic-rate taxpayers who use salary sacrifice:

No matter how much you save, and for how long, and no matter how well your investments perform, you will end up with a 34% bigger pension pot.

In other words, a basic-rate taxpayer who uses salary sacrifice will have 34% more retirement money than someone who does not.

So if your pension pot would have been, say, £100,000 without salary sacrifice, it will be £134,000 with salary sacrifice. If your pension pot would have been £200,000 without salary sacrifice, it will be £268,000 with salary sacrifice. If your pension pot would have been £300,000 without salary sacrifice it will be £402,000 with salary sacrifice... and so on.

When you stop and think about it, the implications are enormous. Salary sacrifice could have a HUGE impact on your quality of life when you retire.

Normally, to achieve a 34% increase in your retirement income you would have to work for several more years or save a bigger percentage of your income.

With salary sacrifice this outcome can be achieved without you or your employer paying a penny: the taxman picks up the entire tab!

So far we've looked at basic-rate taxpayers. Next we'll examine how much better off higher-rate taxpayers are with salary sacrifice arrangements.

Chapter 5

Salary Sacrifice Case Study: Higher-Rate Taxpayer

Introduction

In this chapter we are going to follow the same Jane from Chapters 1 and 2 and show you how she can boost her pension pot with a salary sacrifice arrangement.

Remember Jane earns £60,000 and is a higher-rate taxpayer. Higher-rate taxpayers pay 40% income tax and 2% national insurance on their earnings over £42,475.

Jane's Retirement Savings

We know from Chapter 1 that Jane's income tax and national insurance bill comes to £18,590. She saves £1,800 (3% of her salary) which leaves her with a disposable income of £39,610.

Like John from the previous case study, she also has a family to support and feels she cannot live on a penny less than £39,610.

Jane decides to open a self-invested personal pension (SIPP). She contributes £2,400 and the taxman tops this up with an extra £600 of free cash (her basic-rate tax relief), bringing Jane's total pension saving to £3,000.

Jane can afford to increase the amount she saves from £1,800 to £2,400 because she also receives a £600 income tax refund when she submits her tax return (her higher-rate tax relief).

In summary, Jane saves £3,000 in her SIPP, even though her personal contribution is only £1,800.

The amount she saves has increased by 67%.

Avoiding National Insurance

So far, Jane has enjoyed full *income tax* relief on her pension contributions but no national insurance relief because, as we know, there is no national insurance relief for pension contributions made by employees.

So Jane decides to stop contributing personally and asks her employer to make the contributions directly.

In return, Jane agrees to sacrifice £3,103 of salary which takes her from £60,000 to £56,897 – I will explain why she sacrifices this exact amount in Chapter 6.

After deducting income tax and national insurance she is left with £39,610 – the exact amount we know she needs to live on.

Jane's employer pays the £3,103 of sacrificed salary directly into her pension plan. Her employer also contributes the employer's national insurance saving, which comes to £428 (£3,103 x 13.8%).

Jane's total pension contribution is now £3,531 and has increased by 18%.

It's not as much as the 34% increase enjoyed by John, the basic-rate taxpayer, because higher-rate taxpayers generally only save 2% national insurance on the salary they sacrifice, whereas basic-rate taxpayers save 12%.

Both types of taxpayer, however, can benefit from their employers' 13.8% national insurance saving.

Although Jane's pension contribution hasn't increased as much as John's in percentage terms, it has increased more in pounds and pence.

Her pension contribution has risen by £531, compared with John's rise of £424.

Remember Jane hasn't paid a single penny out of her own pocket to achieve this result!

Total Tax Savings

It is also important to remember that Jane is enjoying much more *income tax* relief than John (40% as opposed to 20%). Remember, before Jane started contributing to a pension plan she was not enjoying any national insurance relief OR income tax relief and was saving just £1,800 per year.

Now she is enjoying full income tax and national insurance relief and the amount she saves is £3,531 – an increase of 96%.

In summary, Jane is avoiding 40% income tax, 2% employee's national insurance and 13.8% employer's national insurance on the money she contributes to her pension plan. She is still left with £39,610 of take-home pay but her retirement saving has increased as follows:

£1,800

No pension

↓

£3,000

Pension with income tax relief
No national insurance relief

↓

£3,531

Pension with income tax relief
<u>and</u> national insurance relief

Jane's Take Home Pay Stays the Same

	Before Salary Sacrifice	After Salary Sacrifice
	£	£
Salary	60,000	56,897
Less:		
Income tax	13,410 *	12,769
National insurance	4,580	4,518
Pension contribution	2,400	0
Disposable income	**39,610**	**39,610**

... But Her Pension Pot Increases By 18%

	Before Salary Sacrifice	After Salary Sacrifice
	£	£
Employee contribution	2,400	-
Taxman's top up	600	-
Employer contribution	-	3,103
Employer's NI saving	-	428
Total	**3,000**	**3,531**

* Reduced by £600 higher-rate income tax relief.

Long-Term Benefits – Higher-Rate Taxpayers

Again, the above example is a one-year snapshot. Pension plans are long-term savings vehicles, so let's examine how salary sacrifice affects Jane's pension pot over a period of 10 years.

The table below shows how Jane's pension pot grows with and without salary sacrifice.

Year	Before Sacrifice £	After Sacrifice £
1	3,000	3,531
2	6,210	7,309
3	9,645	11,352
4	13,320	15,677
5	17,252	20,306
6	21,460	25,258
7	25,962	30,557
8	30,779	36,227
9	35,934	42,294
10	41,449	48,786

The assumptions are the same as for John in the previous case study: Jane's annual pension contribution stays the same each year (£3,000 without salary sacrifice and £3,531 with salary sacrifice) and her investments grow by 7% per year tax free.

In year 10 Jane will have £41,449 in her pension pot without salary sacrifice compared with £48,786 with salary sacrifice.

Again, as with John, what is relevant is the *percentage difference* between the two columns in the table. Every year it is exactly the same: 18%.

This implies the following for higher-rate taxpayers who use salary sacrifice:

No matter how much you save, and for how long, and no matter how well your investments perform, you will end up with an 18% bigger pension pot.

So again salary sacrifice could have a big impact on your quality of life when you retire.

And remember, with salary sacrifice this outcome is achieved without costing you or your employer a penny: the taxman picks up the entire tab.

Chapter 6

Calculating How Much YOU Can Save

So much for John and Jane. In this chapter I am going to show you how to do the number crunching for your personal situation and show you how much better off you could be, in pounds and pence, with a salary sacrifice pension.

There are three steps here:

1. Calculate how much salary you need to sacrifice. This amount will be paid into your pension by your employer. The aim here is to make sure your after-tax disposable income does not decrease.

2. Multiply (1) by 13.8%. This is your employer's national insurance saving and is also added to your pension pot.

3. Compare (1) + (2) with your current gross pension contribution.

The calculation is different for basic-rate taxpayers and higher-rate taxpayers (generally those earning more than £42,475 in the current tax year) because these two groups pay different amounts of income tax and national insurance.

Basic-Rate Taxpayers

Let's say you are a basic-rate taxpayer and personally contribute £100 to your pension plan. To get that £100 in your hands you will have had to earn salary of £147:

£147 _less_ 20% income tax _less_ 12% national insurance = £100

So if you give up £147 of salary *and* stop making pension contributions you will still have exactly the same amount of disposable income.

So, to calculate how much salary you should sacrifice, simply take your current cash pension contribution (the amount you personally contribute, before the taxman tops it up) and add back the 20% income tax and 12% national insurance you have paid.

To do this quickly, simply divide your cash pension contribution by 0.68:

$$\frac{\text{Cash Pension Contribution}}{0.68}$$

Example

John is a basic-rate taxpayer and personally contributes £1,000 to his pension plan annually. His total gross contribution, including the taxman's top up, is £1,250. The amount of salary John needs to sacrifice is calculated as follows:

$$\frac{£1,000}{0.68}$$

$$= £1,471$$

If John stops contributing to his pension plan and sacrifices this amount of salary, his disposable income will remain exactly the same.

His employer will contribute £1,471 to his pension plan plus an extra £203 (£1,471 x 13.8%), representing the employer's national insurance saving. His total pension contribution will be £1,674.

Table 1 shows the same calculation for a whole range of different pension contributions.

The columns can be described as follows:

1) Cash Contribution. Cash pension contribution _before_ the taxman's top up payment is added.

2) Gross Contribution. Found by dividing (1) by 0.8. This is the total gross pension contribution, ie with the taxman's top up payment added.

3) Salary Sacrifice. Found by dividing (1) by 0.68. The amount of salary you should sacrifice to keep your take-home pay constant.

4) New Contribution. This is your new salary sacrifice pension contribution amount, which is simply column (3) plus an extra 13.8%, representing your employer's national insurance saving.

5) Increase. The increase in your pension saving: (4) minus (2). In each case the new pension contribution (4) is 34% higher than the old one (2).

TABLE 1
Sample Pension Increases: Basic-Rate Taxpayers

Cash Contribution (1) £	Gross Contribution (2) £	Salary Sacrifice (3) £	New Contribution (4) £	Increase (5) £
500	625	735	837	212
750	938	1,103	1,255	318
1,000	1,250	1,471	1,674	424
1,250	1,563	1,838	2,092	529
1,500	1,875	2,206	2,510	635
1,750	2,188	2,574	2,929	741
2,000	2,500	2,941	3,347	847
2,250	2,813	3,309	3,765	953
2,500	3,125	3,676	4,184	1,059
2,750	3,438	4,044	4,602	1,165
3,000	3,750	4,412	5,021	1,271
3,500	4,375	5,147	5,857	1,482
4,000	5,000	5,882	6,694	1,694
4,500	5,625	6,618	7,531	1,906
5,000	6,250	7,353	8,368	2,118
5,500	6,875	8,088	9,204	2,329
6,000	7,500	8,824	10,041	2,541
6,500	8,125	9,559	10,878	2,753
7,000	8,750	10,294	11,715	2,965
7,500	9,375	11,029	12,551	3,176
8,000	10,000	11,765	13,388	3,388
8,500	10,625	12,500	14,225	3,600
9,000	11,250	13,235	15,062	3,812
9,500	11,875	13,971	15,899	4,024
10,000	12,500	14,706	16,735	4,235

Column descriptions:

1) **Cash Contribution.** A range of cash pension contributions, before the taxman's top up payment is added.

2) **Gross Contribution.** Found by dividing (1) by 0.8. This is the total gross pension contribution, ie with the taxman's top up payment added.

3) **Salary Sacrifice.** Found by dividing (1) by 0.68. The amount of salary you have to sacrifice while keeping your take-home pay constant.

4) **New Contribution.** This is your new pension contribution which is simply column (3) plus 13.8%, representing the employer's national insurance saving.

5) **Increase.** The increase in pension saving: (4) minus (2).

Let's take a brief look at some of the numbers in the table.

If you are currently personally contributing £2,000 per year to a pension plan, you will be £847 better off with a salary sacrifice pension.

If you are contributing £3,000 per year you will be £1,271 better off, if you are contributing £6,000 per year you will be £2,541 better off... and so on.

If the amount you contribute to your pension plan each year is not shown in Table 1, I hope I have given you the necessary tools to work out how much better off you will be with a salary sacrifice pension.

As a general rule, your pension savings will be 34% higher than before if you are a basic-rate taxpayer.

Your Long-Term Savings – Basic Rate Taxpayer

So much for your *annual* savings. How much better off are you likely to be after a longer period – say 10 years – with a salary sacrifice pension?

Table 2 attempts to answer this question for a whole range of annual pension contributions and illustrates the potential savings in pounds and pence.

It's the fourth column in Table 2 that is the important one – it shows you in pounds and pence how much better off you could be with a salary sacrifice pension after 10 years.

A number of assumptions have been used to crunch the numbers. First, to keep things simple, it is assumed that the amount saved remains the same from year to year.

Second, it is assumed that the pension investments grow by 7% per year. Neither assumption makes a huge amount of difference to the outcome.

TABLE 2
Savings After 10 Years: Basic-Rate Taxpayers

Annual Cash Contribution £	Pension Pot No Sacrifice £	Pension Pot With Sacrifice £	Pension Pot Increase £
500	8,635	11,561	2,926
750	12,953	17,342	4,389
1,000	17,271	23,129	5,858
1,250	21,588	28,903	7,315
1,500	25,906	34,683	8,778
1,750	30,223	40,464	10,240
2,000	34,541	46,244	11,703
2,250	38,859	52,025	13,166
2,500	43,176	57,806	14,629
2,750	47,494	63,586	16,092
3,000	51,812	69,367	17,555
3,500	60,447	80,928	20,481
4,000	69,082	92,489	23,407
4,500	77,718	104,050	26,333
5,000	86,353	115,611	29,258
5,500	94,988	127,172	32,184
6,000	103,623	138,733	35,110
6,500	112,259	150,295	38,036
7,000	120,894	161,856	40,962
7,500	129,529	173,417	43,888
8,000	138,164	184,978	46,813
8,500	146,800	196,539	49,739
9,000	155,435	208,100	52,665
9,500	164,070	219,661	55,591
10,000	172,706	231,222	58,517

Assumptions:

- Pension investments grow by 7% per year
- No increase in annual pension contribution

Let's take a look at a sample number from the table. If you personally contribute £4,000 per year to your pension plan, you will end up with £69,082 after 10 years. But if you have a salary sacrifice pension you will end up with £92,489 – an increase of £23,407.

That's quite a big increase. Remember this money is completely **free**! You would not have to save a single penny extra to enjoy this boost to your retirement savings.

The extra money comes about because you and your employer are saving national insurance.

Ultra Long Term Savings – Basic-Rate Taxpayers

I used a 10 year period in Table 2 because I believe most people do not look much further into the future than this.

In reality, pension plans are often *ultra long-term* savings vehicles and it is possible you will be saving for much longer than 10 years – maybe 20 years, 30 years, 40 years... or even longer!

With this in mind it's important to note that a basic-rate taxpayer (or a couple who are both basic-rate taxpayers) saving £5,000 per year and switching to a salary sacrifice pension will end up with:

- An **extra** £87,000 after 20 years

- An **extra** £200,000 after 30 years

- An **extra** £423,000 after 40 years

In my opinion these results are staggering and the most important numbers in the book if you are a basic-rate taxpayer.

By simply changing the way your pension contributions are paid you could end up with an **extra** £87,000 or even £423,000, without paying a single penny extra into your pension plan.

A pension contribution of £5,000 per year is hardly onerous. For a couple it represents a monthly contribution of around £200 each.

Higher-Rate Taxpayers

In this section I'm going to show you how to do the number crunching for your personal situation if you are a higher-rate taxpayer and show you how much better off you could be, in pounds and pence, with a salary sacrifice pension.

First of all we have to calculate how much salary you should sacrifice so that you end up with exactly the same amount of after-tax disposable income.

Let's say you are a higher-rate taxpayer and personally contribute £100 to your pension plan. We know from Chapter 2 that you will receive £25 of higher-rate relief, so the actual cost to you is just £75.

To get £75 of income in your hands you will have had to earn £129 of salary:

£129 *less* 40% income tax *less* 2% national insurance = £75

So if you sacrifice £129 of salary and stop making pension contributions you will still have exactly the same amount of disposable income to spend.

To perform the same calculation for yourself and calculate exactly how much salary you need to sacrifice just follow these two simple steps:

- **Step 1.** Multiply the amount you personally contribute to your pension by 0.75 – the resulting number is what your pension contributions are actually costing you and takes into account your higher-rate relief.

- **Step 2.** Add back the 40% income tax and 2% national insurance you have paid on this income. To do this divide the result from Step 1 by 0.58:

$$\frac{\text{Step 1}}{0.58}$$

Example

Jane, a higher-rate taxpayer, personally contributes £2,400 per year to her pension. The taxman tops this up with £600, so her gross pension contribution is £3,000. Jane's salary sacrifice is calculated as follows:

- **Step 1.** *Multiply the amount she personally contributes to her pension by 0.75:*

$$£2,400 \times 0.75 = £1,800$$

- **Step 2.** *Add back her 40% income tax and 2% national insurance by dividing the result by 0.58:*

$$£1,800/0.58 = £3,103$$

This is the amount of income Jane has to sacrifice. If she sacrifices £3,103 of salary and stops contributing to her pension plan, her disposable income will remain exactly the same.

Her employer will contribute £3,103 to her pension plan, plus an extra £428 (£3,103 x 13.8%). This is the employer's national insurance saving. Her total pension contribution is now £3,531.

Table 3 shows the same calculation for a whole range of different pension contributions. The columns can be described as follows:

1) Cash Contribution. Cash pension contribution *before* the taxman's top up payment is added.

2) Total Contribution. Found by dividing (1) by 0.8. This is the gross pension contribution, ie with taxman's top up added.

3) Salary Sacrifice. Found by dividing the pension contribution net of all tax relief by 0.58 – the amount of salary a higher-rate taxpayer has to sacrifice while keeping take-home pay constant.

4) New Contribution. This is your new salary sacrifice pension contribution amount, which is simply column (3) plus an extra 13.8%, representing the employer's national insurance saving.

5) Increase. The increase in pension saving: (4) minus (2). In each case the new pension contribution (4) is 18% higher than the old one (2).

TABLE 3
Sample Pension Increases: Higher-Rate Taxpayers

Cash Contribution (1) £	Total Contribution (2) £	Salary Sacrifice (3) £	New Contribution (4) £	Increase (5) £
500	625	647	736	111
750	938	970	1,104	166
1,000	1,250	1,293	1,472	222
1,250	1,563	1,616	1,839	277
1,500	1,875	1,940	2,207	332
1,750	2,188	2,263	2,575	388
2,000	2,500	2,586	2,943	443
2,250	2,813	2,909	3,311	498
2,500	3,125	3,233	3,679	554
2,750	3,438	3,556	4,047	609
3,000	3,750	3,879	4,415	665
3,500	4,375	4,526	5,150	775
4,000	5,000	5,172	5,886	886
4,500	5,625	5,819	6,622	997
5,000	6,250	6,466	7,358	1,108
5,500	6,875	7,112	8,094	1,219
6,000	7,500	7,759	8,829	1,329
6,500	8,125	8,405	9,565	1,440
7,000	8,750	9,052	10,301	1,551
7,500	9,375	9,698	11,037	1,662
8,000	10,000	10,345	11,772	1,772
8,500	10,625	10,991	12,508	1,883
9,000	11,250	11,638	13,244	1,994
9,500	11,875	12,284	13,980	2,105
10,000	12,500	12,931	14,716	2,216
10,500	13,125	13,578	15,451	2,326
11,000	13,750	14,224	16,187	2,437
11,500	14,375	14,871	16,923	2,548
12,000	15,000	15,517	17,659	2,659
12,500	15,625	16,164	18,394	2,769
13,000	16,250	16,810	19,130	2,880
13,500	16,875	17,457	19,866	2,991
14,000	17,500	18,103	20,602	3,102
14,500	18,125	18,750	21,338	3,213
15,000	18,750	19,397	22,073	3,323
16,000	20,000	20,690	23,545	3,545
17,000	21,250	21,983	25,016	3,766
18,000	22,500	23,276	26,488	3,988
19,000	23,750	24,569	27,959	4,209
20,000	25,000	25,862	29,431	4,431

The table is easy to use. For example, if you are currently personally contributing £6,000 per year to your pension plan, you will be £1,329 better off with a salary sacrifice pension.

There are two important points to remember about this table:

- First, you will enjoy this free increase to you pension pot **every year.**

- Second, this is just your national insurance saving. As a higher-rate taxpayer you will also be enjoying 40% income tax relief on your pension contributions.

  For example, a higher-rate taxpayer who personally contributes £6,000 to a pension plan will receive a £1,500 income tax refund from the taxman so the actual cost is just £4,500. The taxman's top-up will take the total pension contribution to £7,500. With salary sacrifice the pension contribution then goes up to £8,829 without costing you a penny extra.

  So what you have is a pension contribution of £8,829 that has effectively cost just £4,500.

Your Long-Term Savings – Higher Rate Taxpayers

So much for your *annual* savings. How much better off are you likely to be after a longer period – say 10 years – with a salary sacrifice pension?

Table 4 attempts to answer this question for a whole range of annual pension contributions and illustrates the potential savings in pounds and pence for a higher-rate taxpayer.

It's the fourth column in Table 4 that is the important one – it shows you in pounds and pence how much better off you could be with a salary sacrifice pension after 10 years.

Again a number of assumptions have been used to crunch the numbers. First, to keep things simple, it is assumed that the amount saved remains the same from year to year. Second, it is assumed that the pension investments grow by 7% per year. Neither assumption makes a huge amount of difference to the outcome.

Let's take a look at a sample number from the table. If you personally contribute £6,000 per year to your pension plan, you will end up with £103,623 after 10 years. But if you have a salary sacrifice pension you will end up with £121,990 – an increase of £18,367.

That's quite a big increase. Remember this money is completely **free**! You would not have to save a single penny extra to enjoy this boost to your retirement savings.

The extra money comes about because you and your employer are saving national insurance.

TABLE 4
Savings After 10 Years: Higher-Rate Taxpayers

Annual Cash Contribution £	Pension Pot No Sacrifice £	Pension Pot With Sacrifice £	Pension Pot Increase £
500	8,635	10,166	1,531
750	12,953	15,249	2,296
1,000	17,271	20,332	3,061
1,250	21,588	25,415	3,826
1,500	25,906	30,497	4,592
1,750	30,223	35,580	5,357
2,000	34,541	40,663	6,122
2,250	38,859	45,746	6,887
2,500	43,176	50,829	7,653
2,750	47,494	55,912	8,418
3,000	51,812	60,995	9,183
3,500	60,447	71,161	10,714
4,000	69,082	81,326	12,244
4,500	77,718	91,492	13,775
5,000	86,353	101,658	15,305
5,500	94,988	111,824	16,836
6,000	103,623	121,990	18,367
6,500	112,259	132,156	19,897
7,000	120,894	142,321	21,427
7,500	129,529	152,487	22,958
8,000	138,164	162,653	24,488
8,500	146,800	172,819	26,019
9,000	155,435	182,985	27,550
9,500	164,070	193,150	29,080
10,000	172,706	203,316	30,611
10,500	181,341	213,482	32,141
11,000	189,976	223,648	33,672
11,500	198,611	233,814	35,202
12,000	207,247	243,979	36,733
12,500	215,882	254,145	38,263
13,000	224,517	264,311	39,794
13,500	233,153	274,477	41,324
14,000	241,788	284,643	42,855
14,500	250,423	294,808	44,385
15,000	259,058	304,974	45,916
16,000	276,329	325,306	48,977
17,000	293,600	345,638	52,038
18,000	310,870	365,969	55,099
19,000	328,141	386,301	58,160
20,000	345,411	406,632	61,221

Ultra Long Term Savings – Higher-Rate Taxpayers

I used a 10 year period to construct Table 4.

Of course pension plans are ultra long-term savings vehicles and it is possible you will be saving for longer than 10 years – maybe 20 years, 30 years, or 40 years.

With this in mind it's interesting to note that a higher-rate taxpayer saving £7,500 per year who switches to a salary sacrifice pension will end up with:

- An **extra** £68,000 after 20 years

- An **extra** £157,000 after 30 years

- An **extra** £332,000 after 40 years

These are probably the most important numbers in this guide if you are a higher-rate taxpayer.

Again, I find these results staggering. By simply changing the way your pension contributions are paid you could end up with an **extra** £68,000 or even £332,000, without paying a single penny extra into your pension plan.

A pension contribution of £7,500 per year is hardly onerous. For a couple who are both higher-rate taxpayers it represents a monthly contribution of just over £300 each.

Chapter 7

High Income Earners

In this chapter we are going to take a closer look at how much better off high income earners will be with a salary sacrifice pension.

There are two groups of high earners that are special cases:

- Those earning over £100,000
- Those earning over £150,000

Income between £100,000 and £114,950

When your income rises above £100,000 your income tax personal allowance – currently £7,475 – is gradually taken away. For every £1 you earn over £100,000, 50p of personal allowance is taken away.

So when your income reaches £114,950 you will have no personal allowance left and your tax bill will have increased by an additional £2,990 (£7,475 x 40%).

What this means is that those earning between £100,000 and £114,950 face a marginal tax rate of 62% (60% income tax plus 2% national insurance).

When you add the 13.8% national insurance paid by the employer, the total tax rate is 75.8% -- a truly 1970s style tax rate!

Example

Colin earns a salary of £100,000 and receives a pay increase of £14,950. This increases his tax bill by £9,269:

- *42% income tax and national insurance – £6,279*
- *Loss of personal allowance – £2,990*

The effective tax rate is 62%:

$$£9,269/£14,950 = 62\%$$

After paying tax Colin is left with just £5,681 of his £14,950 pay increase.

His employer is also straddled with a national insurance bill of £2,063, bringing the total tax bill on the pay rise to £11,332:

$$£11,332/£14,950 = 75.8\%$$

Colin and others in this income group can avoid this penal tax rate by contributing to a pension plan. A salary sacrifice arrangement will further enhance the savings.

Example – Salary Sacrifice

Colin sacrifices £14,950 of salary and his employer contributes this amount into Colin's pension plan.

His employer also contributes the employer's national insurance saving of £2,063 (£14,950 x 13.8%) into the pension plan.

The total amount invested in Colin's pension plan is £17,013.

Remember, before making the salary sacrifice pension contribution Colin was left with just £5,681 of his £14,950 pay increase.

Now he has £17,013 sitting in his pension plan.

Colin has not only recouped the 62% income tax and national insurance payable on his salary increase, he has also recouped the 13.8% national insurance paid by his employer!

Income over £150,000

The Government announced in October 2010 that it was reversing a previous restriction on pension contributions made by those who earn over £150,000.

From 6th April 2011 all pension contributions attract tax relief at the individual's marginal tax rate.

This means contributing to a pension plan will become more attractive than ever for those who earn over £150,000.

These individuals currently face a marginal income tax rate of 50%, so any income they can divert into a pension plan will escape this extortionate tax rate.

Further national insurance savings can be enjoyed if these pension contributions are made via a salary sacrifice arrangement.

Example – Before Salary Sacrifice

Connie earns a salary of £150,000 and receives a pay increase of £10,000. This increases her total income tax and national insurance bill by £5,200 (£10,000 x 52%), leaving her with just £4,800 to take home.

Her employer also pays national insurance of £1,380, bringing the total tax bill on the pay rise to £6,580 for an effective tax rate of almost 66%:

$$£6,580/£10,000 = 65.8\%$$

Example – After Salary Sacrifice

Connie sacrifices £10,000 of salary and her employer contributes this amount into her pension plan.

Her employer also contributes the employer's national insurance saving of £1,380 (£10,000 x 13.8%).

The total amount invested in Connie's pension plan is £11,380.

Before making the salary sacrifice pension contribution, Connie was left with £4,800 out of her £10,000 pay increase. Now she has £11,380 sitting in her pension plan – almost two and a half times more money.

50% Tax May Disappear in 2013

In the March 2011 Budget the Chancellor of the Exchequer gave the clearest indication yet that the 50% income tax rate applying to those who earn over £150,000 will be abolished in the near future:

"I am clear that the 50 pence tax rate would do lasting damage to our economy if it were to become permanent. That is why I regard it as a temporary measure."

Thankfully, the Government realises that high tax rates result in lower tax collections!

No clear timetable has been provided for its removal but many commentators expect it to be abolished in the 2013 Budget.

This has several tax planning implications for high income earners. For example, you may want to consider upping your pension contributions over the next two tax years to take advantage of 50% tax relief.

Summary – High Income Earners

In summary, high income earners have the most to gain from making pension contributions.

If the contributions are made via a salary sacrifice arrangement it is possible to end up with over twice as much money sitting in your pension pot than by taking the income as regular taxed pay.

Chapter 8

The Alternative Way: Boosting Your Pay

In this chapter we are going to show how salary sacrifice pensions can be used to increase your *take home pay*, instead of your pension contributions.

We will follow the same John and Jane from previous chapters to illustrate the potential savings.

Salary Sacrifice Pay Rise – Basic-rate Taxpayer

Before his salary sacrifice John had a salary of £30,000. His take-home pay was £21,762 and he had £1,250 in his pension pot.

John decides that he doesn't want to increase his pension contributions but would like to have more income to cover his household bills.

So he decides to sacrifice £1,098 of salary and his employer contributes this amount to his pension plan. His employer also adds an extra £152 (£1,098 x 13.8%), representing the employer's national insurance saving.

So John ends up with exactly the same amount – £1,250 – sitting in his pension plan.

And what about his take-home pay? John's salary sacrifice takes his salary from £30,000 to £28,902. After deducting income tax and national insurance he is left with £22,016 – an effective increase of £254 in his disposable income.

The number crunching is illustrated in the table below:

John's Take Home Pay Increases by £254

	Before Salary Sacrifice	After Salary Sacrifice
	£	£
Salary	30,000	28,902
Less:		
Income tax	4,505	4,285
National insurance	2,733	2,601
Pension contribution	1,000	0
Disposable income	**21,762**	**22,016**

... And His Pension Pot Stays Exactly the Same

	Before Salary Sacrifice	After Salary Sacrifice
	£	£
Employee contribution	1,000	-
Taxman's top up	250	-
Employer contribution	-	1,098
Employer's NI saving	-	152
Total	**1,250**	**1,250**

Salary Sacrifice Pay Rise – Higher-rate Taxpayer

Before her salary sacrifice Jane had a salary of £60,000. Her take-home pay was £39,610 and she had £3,000 in her pension pot.

Jane decides that she doesn't want to increase her pension contributions but would like to have more income to support her family.

So she decides to sacrifice £2,636 of salary and her employer contributes this amount to her pension plan. Her employer also adds an extra £364 (£2,636 x 13.8%), representing the employer's national insurance saving.

So Jane ends up with exactly the same amount – £3,000 – sitting in her pension plan.

And what about her take-home pay? Jane's salary sacrifice takes her salary from £60,000 to £57,364. After deducting income tax and national insurance she is left with £39,880 – an effective pay increase of £270.

The number crunching is illustrated on the next page.

Jane's Take Home Pay Increases By £270

	Before Salary Sacrifice £	After Salary Sacrifice £
Salary	60,000	57,364
Less:		
Income tax	13,410 *	12,956
National insurance	4,580	4,528
Pension contribution	2,400	0
Disposable income	**39,610**	**39,880**

... And Her Pension Pot Stays Exactly the Same

	Before Salary Sacrifice £	After Salary Sacrifice £
Employee contribution	2,400	-
Taxman's top up	600	-
Employer contribution	-	2,636
Employer's NI saving	-	364
Total	**3,000**	**3,000**

* Reduced by £600 higher-rate income tax relief.

Salary Sacrifice Pay Rise – Your Own Calculation

If you want to increase your take home pay – instead of increasing your pension pot – the key is to sacrifice a smaller amount of salary.

The exact amount of salary you should sacrifice can be found by dividing your current *gross* pension contribution by 1.138.

(Remember your gross pension contribution is the amount sitting in your pension plan and includes the taxman's top up. It is found by dividing your actual cash contribution by 0.8).

This ensures that, when your employer's national insurance saving is added, your pension contribution remains exactly the same but your take-home pay will be higher.

Example

Jane's pre-sacrifice gross pension contribution is £3,000. How much salary should she sacrifice is she wants to save the same amount for retirement but enjoy an increase in her after-tax disposable income?

Her salary sacrifice will be:

$$£3,000/1.138 = £2,636$$

Her employer's national insurance saving will be:

$$£2,636 \times 13.8\% = £364$$

Both amounts are paid into her pension plan resulting in a total pension contribution of £3,000 – exactly the same as before.

Chapter 9

How to Convince Your Employer

After 22 years in the tax publishing business one thing I have learnt is that most tax loopholes come with a catch.

For example, capital gains are taxed much more leniently than income... but you have to take more risks to get them.

You can cut your tax bill to zero by emigrating to a tax haven... but you may not enjoy living in one.

There are several tax shelters that offer mouth-watering tax breaks... but they tie up your money for several years.

And so on...

With salary sacrifice pensions the catch is you need your employer's co-operation. A salary sacrifice pension arrangement will only work if your employer agrees to do the necessary paperwork (see Chapter 11), reduce your salary and contribute to your pension plan.

How much bargaining power you have with your employer will, of course, depend on how big the company is and how senior you are.

If you are a senior executive at a small or medium-sized company, you should find it relatively easy to get your employer to introduce a salary sacrifice arrangement. If you are a junior employee at a multinational corporation your chances are probably slim.

However, because a salary sacrifice arrangement could increase your pension pot by tens of thousands of pounds and have a huge impact on your quality of life when you retire, I believe it's worth fighting for tooth and nail.

Remember, to implement a salary sacrifice arrangement it is NOT necessary for your employer to set up some sort of company pension scheme.

Salary sacrifice works with almost all pension plans including:

- Self-invested personal pensions (SIPPs)
- Personal pensions (group and individual plans)
- Stakeholder pensions (group and individual plans)
- Occupational pension schemes

Fortunately, there are several arguments you can use to convince your employer:

Argument #1 Other Employers Are Doing It

Salary sacrifice pensions are available from some of the country's biggest and most reputable companies, universities and other organisations, including BT, Tesco and the BBC. To stay competitive in the jobs market your employer should also be offering this benefit.

Argument #2 It Has the Taxman's Approval

Salary sacrifice pensions have the taxman's full blessing. In fact, HM Revenue & Customs has even published guidance notes on how to go about it the correct way (see Appendix 2).

Argument #3 It is Easy to Implement

As we will see in Chapter 11, your employer will have to dot a few i's and cross a few t's but the paperwork is all relatively straightforward and only has to be done once.

Argument #4 Mandatory Employer Pensions Are Coming

In the October 2010 spending review the Government confirmed that it is pressing ahead with plans to introduce compulsory pensions for ALL employees.

A state-sponsored pension scheme called NEST (National Employment Savings Trust) will be made available to employers, especially small employers, who do not have their own pension scheme.

Starting in October 2012 employers with 120,000 or more staff will have to start enrolling staff into a pension plan. By July 2014 this requirement will be extended to employers with more than 50 staff and by September 2016 compulsory enrolment will be extended to all employers.

Employers will also be forced to make contributions into the pension scheme, starting at 1% (on a band of earnings) and rising to 3% in October 2017. Employees will have to contribute 1% rising to up to 5%, including tax relief.

For those affected this is an important development. In terms of convincing your employer to offer salary sacrifice, you could point out that introducing a salary sacrifice scheme now could save the employer money in future years.

How? If your employer starts making pension contributions on your behalf now (funded by you via a salary sacrifice) he may not have to make any extra payments (out of his own pocket) when compulsory contributions are eventually introduced.

Argument #5 Giving Employees a FREE Pay Increase

This is by far the most powerful argument you can use to convince your employer to introduce a salary sacrifice pension arrangement.

Salary sacrifice arrangements can be structured so that the employee's pension contributions go up with take-home pay staying exactly the same. Or they can be structured with pension contributions staying the same but take home pay going up (see Chapter 8).

Either way, the employee effectively receives a pay increase that doesn't cost the employer anything. The taxman foots the entire bill.

What rational employer would turn down such an opportunity?

Sharing the Savings with Your Employer

If you are struggling to convince your employer to introduce a salary sacrifice pension arrangement, as a last resort you can offer to share the national insurance savings.

Remember there are two types of national insurance: the type the employee pays and the type the employer pays.

In all the examples so far we have assumed that both the employee's and employer's national insurance savings are paid into the employee's pension plan.

However, to convince your employer to introduce a salary sacrifice pension arrangement you may have to appeal to his selfish side and offer to share the national insurance savings.

Your employer pays 13.8% national insurance on every penny you earn over £7,075. It may be necessary to offer your employer, say, half of the employer's national insurance saving (6.9% of the salary sacrifice amount) to cooperate with you.

Ideally you should negotiate to have your employer share the national insurance savings for just one year, perhaps to compensate him for time spent doing the necessary paperwork.

However, even if your employer is greedy and insists on a permanent national insurance share, you will still be far better off in most cases with a salary sacrifice pension arrangement.

Table 5 illustrates the annual benefit of a salary sacrifice arrangement for a whole range of different pension contribution amounts for basic-rate taxpayers.

The table is exactly the same as Table 1 in Chapter 6, except for columns 4 and 5. In column 4 only half the employer's national insurance saving is added to the employee's pension plan (6.9% instead of 13.8%).

Column 5 is the important one and shows how much better off a basic-rate taxpayer will be every year with a salary sacrifice arrangement if only half the employer's national insurance saving is paid into the pension plan.

For example, an employee who contributes £4,000 per year to a pension plan will still be £1,288 better off *every year* with a salary sacrifice arrangement (the same employee was £1,694 better off when all of the employer's national insurance saving was paid into the pension plan).

If you compare column 4 (the new salary sacrifice pension contribution) with column 2 (pension contribution before salary sacrifice) you will find that:

No matter how much basic-rate taxpayers contribute to a pension plan, they will still end up with 26% more money with a salary sacrifice arrangement... even if only half the employer's national insurance saving is paid into the pension plan.

TABLE 5
Sharing National Insurance Savings with the Employer:
Sample Pension Increases: Basic-Rate Taxpayers

Cash Contribution (1) £	Gross Contribution (2) £	Salary Sacrifice (3) £	New Contribution (4) £	Increase (5) £
500	625	735	786	161
750	938	1,103	1,179	242
1,000	1,250	1,471	1,572	322
1,250	1,563	1,838	1,965	403
1,500	1,875	2,206	2,358	483
1,750	2,188	2,574	2,751	564
2,000	2,500	2,941	3,144	644
2,250	2,813	3,309	3,537	725
2,500	3,125	3,676	3,930	805
2,750	3,438	4,044	4,323	886
3,000	3,750	4,412	4,716	966
3,500	4,375	5,147	5,502	1,127
4,000	5,000	5,882	6,288	1,288
4,500	5,625	6,618	7,074	1,449
5,000	6,250	7,353	7,860	1,610
5,500	6,875	8,088	8,646	1,771
6,000	7,500	8,824	9,432	1,932
6,500	8,125	9,559	10,218	2,093
7,000	8,750	10,294	11,004	2,254
7,500	9,375	11,029	11,790	2,415
8,000	10,000	11,765	12,576	2,576
8,500	10,625	12,500	13,363	2,738
9,000	11,250	13,235	14,149	2,899
9,500	11,875	13,971	14,935	3,060
10,000	12,500	14,706	15,721	3,221

Column descriptions:

1) Cash Contribution. A range of cash pension contributions, before the taxman's top up payment is added.

2) Gross Contribution. Found by dividing (1) by 0.8. This is the total gross pension contribution, ie with the taxman's top up payment added.

3) Salary Sacrifice. Found by dividing (1) by 0.68. The amount of salary you have to sacrifice while keeping your take-home pay constant.

4) New Contribution. This is simply column (3) plus 6.9%, representing **half** the employer's national insurance saving.

5) Increase. The increase in pension saving: (4) minus (2).

Higher Rate Taxpayers

Table 6 illustrates the annual benefit of a salary sacrifice arrangement for a whole range of different pension contribution amounts for *higher-rate taxpayers*.

The table is exactly the same as Table 3 in Chapter 6, except for columns 4 and 5. In column 4 only half the employer's national insurance saving is added to the employee's pension plan (6.9% instead of 13.8%).

Column 5 is the important one and shows how much better off a higher-rate taxpayer will be every year with a salary sacrifice arrangement, if only half the employer's national insurance saving is paid into his pension plan.

For example, an employee who contributes £6,000 per year to a pension plan will be £794 better off every year with a salary sacrifice arrangement (the same employee was £1,329 better off when all of the employer's national insurance saving was paid into the pension plan).

If you compare column 4 (the new salary sacrifice pension contribution) with column 2 (pension contribution before salary sacrifice) you will find that:

No matter how much higher-rate taxpayers contribute to a pension plan, they will still end up with 11% more money with a salary sacrifice arrangement... even if only half the employer's national insurance saving is paid into the pension plan.

TABLE 6
Sharing National Insurance Savings with the Employer:
Sample Pension Increases: Higher-Rate Taxpayers

Cash Contribution (1)	Total Contribution (2)	Salary Sacrifice (3)	New Contribution (4)	Increase (5)
£	£	£	£	£
500	625	647	691	66
750	938	970	1,037	99
1,000	1,250	1,293	1,382	132
1,250	1,563	1,616	1,728	165
1,500	1,875	1,940	2,073	198
1,750	2,188	2,263	2,419	232
2,000	2,500	2,586	2,765	265
2,250	2,813	2,909	3,110	298
2,500	3,125	3,233	3,456	331
2,750	3,438	3,556	3,801	364
3,000	3,750	3,879	4,147	397
3,500	4,375	4,526	4,838	463
4,000	5,000	5,172	5,529	529
4,500	5,625	5,819	6,220	595
5,000	6,250	6,466	6,912	662
5,500	6,875	7,112	7,603	728
6,000	7,500	7,759	8,294	794
6,500	8,125	8,405	8,985	860
7,000	8,750	9,052	9,676	926
7,500	9,375	9,698	10,367	992
8,000	10,000	10,345	11,059	1,059
8,500	10,625	10,991	11,750	1,125
9,000	11,250	11,638	12,441	1,191
9,500	11,875	12,284	13,132	1,257
10,000	12,500	12,931	13,823	1,323
11,000	13,750	14,224	15,206	1,456
12,000	15,000	15,517	16,588	1,588
13,000	16,250	16,810	17,970	1,720
14,000	17,500	18,103	19,353	1,853
15,000	18,750	19,397	20,735	1,985
16,000	20,000	20,690	22,117	2,117
17,000	21,250	21,983	23,500	2,250
18,000	22,500	23,276	24,882	2,382
19,000	23,750	24,569	26,264	2,514
20,000	25,000	25,862	27,647	2,647

Employer Refuses to Share NI Savings

What happens if your employer refuses to share any of his national insurance savings?

This is the worst case scenario but cannot be ruled out.

If you are a basic-rate taxpayer a salary sacrifice pension is still worth having because your pension contributions will still be approximately 18% higher.

If you are a higher-rate taxpayer, however, a salary sacrifice pension will increase your pension contributions by a paltry 3%.

Remember, higher-rate taxpayers only pay 2% national insurance on earnings over £42,475. So a salary sacrifice saves them very little unless some or all of the employer's much larger 13.8% national insurance bill is also added to the pension pot.

In summary, a salary sacrifice arrangement loses most of its attractiveness if you are a higher-rate taxpayer and your employer refuses to share his national insurance savings.

Summary

- A salary sacrifice arrangement requires your employer's approval.

- To convince your employer to introduce salary sacrifice you can use the following arguments:

    - Many big, reputable employers offer salary sacrifice
    - It has the taxman's approval
    - It is easy to implement
    - Mandatory employer pensions are coming
    - Salary sacrifice allows employer to give employees a FREE pay increase

- If these arguments do not work you can offer to share the national insurance savings with your employer.

- A basic-rate taxpayer who agrees to share the national insurance savings with the employer could still end up with a 26% bigger pension pot.

- A higher-rate taxpayer who agrees to share the national insurance savings with the employer could still end up with an 11% bigger pension pot.

- If your employer refuses to share any of his national insurance savings, a salary sacrifice arrangement is still worthwhile if you are a basic-rate taxpayer... but not very effective if you are a higher-rate taxpayer.

Chapter 10

The Drawbacks

With salary sacrifice pensions your gross salary is reduced, so anything that depends on your gross salary could be affected, including your:

- Employment benefits
- Borrowing ability
- Basic state pension
- State second pension (S2P)
- Maternity pay

Employment Benefits

If a salary sacrifice reduces your gross salary then this could *potentially* also reduce your:

- Future pay increases
- Overtime
- Life insurance cover provided by your employer
- Redundancy payments

I put the word 'potentially' in italics because most salary sacrifice arrangements address this issue by making sure all benefits are based on the employee's original salary – also known as the 'reference salary' or 'notional salary'.

So if you are currently earning £40,000 and your salary is reduced to £37,000, your employment benefits can be calculated on the basis that you are still earning £40,000.

One potential issue concerns refunds of employee pension contributions. If you currently belong to an occupational pension scheme and leave the company with less than two years service, you may be entitled to a refund of the pension contributions you have made personally.

However, pension contributions made by your employer to an occupational pension scheme as part of a salary sacrifice arrangement are not employee contributions and may not be refunded.

Borrowing Ability

Any salary reduction could affect your ability to borrow money, for example to buy a house or for any other purpose.

One solution is for your employer to provide the lender with a letter of reference confirming your reference salary.

For example, many of the university salary sacrifice documents state that:

"You should quote your current annual salary on mortgage applications and your payslip will substantiate this figure as your annual salary. If The University Payroll Office receives requests for mortgage references from lenders they will quote your current salary i.e. before the reduction."

This potential issue can therefore be addressed. However, there is still a potential risk that some lenders will not accept your reference salary and use the lower post-sacrifice salary.

Basic State Pension

It is very unlikely that sacrificing some salary will affect your basic state pension entitlement. Your basic state pension is based on the number of years you have worked, not the amount of national insurance you have paid or the level of your salary.

Those on very low incomes have to be careful, however. If you earn less than the 'lower earnings limit' (LEL) in any year, that year will not be included in your contribution record when your basic state pension entitlement is calculated.

For the 2011/12 tax year the LEL is £5,304.

Other state benefits are also affected if your income falls below the LEL, including statutory sick pay, maternity pay, incapacity benefit and jobseekers allowance.

The general consensus among pension experts is that you should not participate in a salary sacrifice arrangement if your income will fall below the LEL.

(Also remember that your employer cannot let a salary sacrifice take you under the national minimum wage.)

For everyone else, as long as you have a full national insurance history, you will receive the full basic state pension when you reach the state pension age.

State Pension Basics

The state pension age is rising to 66 in 2020 for both men and women. There are also proposals to keep increasing the state pension age, as longevity increases in the years ahead.

Although this is unwelcome news it comes as no surprise to those who understand how the state pension is funded. State pensions are not paid out of a big pot of money. Rather, the state pension system is really just a giant Ponzi scheme: Those who are currently working pay the pensions of those who are retired.

The problem is that, with every year that passes, there are more people taking money out and fewer people putting money in!

At present there are four people of working age for every person over the state pension age. By 2050 there could be just two people of working age for every retired person.

Calculating Your Basic State Pension

How much basic state pension you receive currently depends on how many qualifying years you have built up. Qualifying years are years in which you pay, or are treated as having paid, national insurance.

From 6th April 2011, to qualify for a full basic state pension you need 30 qualifying years.

For 2011/12 the maximum basic state pension for a single person is £5,312 per year and for married couples it is £8,494.

The basic state pension is indexed each year for those living in the UK, countries in the European Union, the US and certain other countries.

However, more than half a million UK pensioners who have retired abroad do not enjoy any increases. These includes retirees in Australia, Canada, Dubai, Hong Kong, India, New Zealand, Nigeria, Pakistan, Singapore, South Africa, Thailand, many Caribbean islands (except Barbados, Bermuda, and Jamaica), and Zimbabwe.

To obtain your very own state pension forecast go to:

www.direct.gov.uk/en/Pensionsandretirementplanning/StatePension

State Second Pension (S2P)

Your state second pension IS currently based on your gross salary, so sacrificing some salary *may* reduce your entitlement.

I say 'may' because it all depends on how much you earn.

Even if your state second pension is reduced, in many cases the reduction will be tiny relative to the benefits you will enjoy from the salary sacrifice arrangement.

Furthermore, the way the state second pension is calculated is changing – possibly radically – and these changes may limit any adverse impact from salary sacrifice arrangements in the future.

Having said all that, it is necessary to include a disclaimer here. Because it is impossible to predict what will happen to the state second pension in the future, it is difficult to provide a cast iron guarantee that your entitlement will not be adversely affected by a salary sacrifice.

Calculating the State Second Pension

Most people don't know how their state second pension is calculated, so it's worth explaining briefly.

You build up your entitlement year by year. The amount added to your state pension account for the current 2011/12 tax year is based on your earnings for the current year, using the following scale:

Earnings	%
Below £5,304	0
£5,304-£14,400	40
£14,400-£40,040	10
Above £40,040	0

I'll explain how the table works shortly but first it is possible to make some general comments about how a salary sacrifice arrangement could affect your S2P entitlement:

- The first 0% figure in the table means that you accrue no S2P entitlement at all if your income is less than £5,304. So if a salary sacrifice takes your income below £5,304 you will lose your S2P entitlement for the current year.

  (This reinforces our recommendation earlier that those earning less than £5,304 should probably steer clear of salary sacrifice arrangements.)

- The second 0% figure means that you accrue no additional S2P entitlement on earnings over £40,040 (known as the upper accrual point). In other words, those earning above £40,040 get S2P based on £40,040.

  This implies that:

  If your earnings both before and after a salary sacrifice are over £40,040, your S2P entitlement will not be affected.

This means that Jane, our higher-rate taxpayer from earlier chapters will not be affected. Her earnings both before and after the salary sacrifice are over £40,040.

- If you earn between £5,304 and £14,400 (known as the lower earnings threshold) you are automatically treated as having earnings of £14,400. (The Government introduced this rule to help those on low incomes).

This means that:

If your earnings both before and after a salary sacrifice are between £5,304 and £14,400, your S2P entitlement will not be affected.

Those who *are* likely to be adversely affected by a salary sacrifice arrangement include the following:

- If your earnings both before and after a salary sacrifice are between £14,400 and £40,040. In this band your S2P accrual is based on your *actual earnings* so any reduction in your earnings will reduce your S2P accrual.

- A salary sacrifice causes your earnings to fall from one earnings band to another. For example, if your earnings fall from above £14,400 to below £14,400 you will lose your 10% accrual altogether for the current year. Similarly if your earnings fall from above £40,040 to below £40,040 you will lose some of your 10% accrual.

The next question is, how severely affected by salary sacrifice is your state second pension likely to be, if you are one of the affected groups? This question is best answered with an example explaining how the state second pension is calculated:

Example – Before Salary Sacrifice

John earns £30,000 a year and has a working life of 49 years (the number of years normally used in this calculation).

Using the above table we calculate his S2P entitlement for the current year as follows:

40% band: (£14,400 less £5,304) = £9,096
10% band: (£30,000 less £14,400) = £15,600

£9,096 x 40%/49 = £74
£15,600 x 10%/49 = £32

Total: £106

What this means is that, when John retires, he will receive a state second pension of £106 per year, based on his earnings for the current 2011/12 tax year. This is just one year, of course, and there will be additional entitlement in respect of previous and future tax years.

The amount he will actually receive when he retires will be adjusted upwards with wage inflation but I have ignored this fact to keep the number crunching simple.

Example – After Salary Sacrifice

John sacrifices some salary and now earns £28,529 a year.

His S2P entitlement for the current year is as follows:

40% band – (£14,400 less £5,304) = £9,056
10% band – (£28,529 less £14,400) = £14,129

£9,056 x 40%/49 = £74
£14,129 x 10%/49 = £29

Total: £103

What this means is that this year's salary sacrifice has reduced John's S2P entitlement by £3 per year. This is weighed against the benefits – a pension pot increase of £424.

State Second Pension – Future Changes

The way the state second pension is calculated is changing and some of these changes may reduce any potential harm caused by salary sacrifice. In particular, a simple flat-rate second pension will eventually be introduced which will not depend on how much you earn.

This change to the way S2P is accrued is currently taking place as follows:

- The £40,040 upper accrual point has been fixed at this amount and will not be increased with inflation. Because the amount will gradually lose value, this change will reduce the earnings-related part of S2P.

- With the £14,400 lower earnings threshold rising each year and the upper accrual point fixed at £40,040, the 10% accrual rate will eventually disappear and S2P will be a flat rate benefit.

State Pensions – Long-term Changes

The Government recently announced that it is planning a radical overhaul of the entire state pension system and in April 2011 the Department for Work and Pensions published a consultation document: *A state pension for the 21st century.*

The current basic state pension and state second pension could be scrapped and replaced with a single flat payment of up to £140 per week for those with a full 30-year national insurance record.

Such a change would potentially make salary sacrifice arrangements more attractive (remember sacrificing salary can reduce your entitlement to the state second pension, which is partly based on your earnings).

Whether this proposal will actually be implemented and in what form remains to be seen.

Maternity Pay

A salary sacrifice arrangement could reduce the amount of statutory maternity pay (SMP) to which you are entitled.

Statutory maternity pay is based on your contractual earnings which count for national insurance contributions. So if your earnings have been reduced because you sacrificed some salary, the amount of statutory maternity pay you receive may also be reduced.

If a salary sacrifice reduces your salary below the lower earnings limit (£5,304 in 2011/12), you will lose your entitlement to receive statutory maternity pay altogether.

How is Statutory Maternity Pay Calculated?

Women are entitled to 52 weeks of maternity leave and 39 weeks of statutory maternity pay.

For the first six weeks you are entitled to receive 90% of your average gross weekly earnings, with no upper limit.

So, clearly, a salary sacrifice could reduce the amount of SMP you receive for the first six weeks.

For the remaining 33 weeks you are entitled to receive the *lesser* of:

- £128.73 per week
- 90% of your average earnings

All except the lowest paid will receive a flat amount of £128.73 per week for this 33 week period, so a salary sacrifice will probably have no effect on this part of your SMP entitlement.

Statutory Maternity Pay – Effect on the Employer

Employers are liable to pay statutory maternity pay but can get most of it refunded.

If the employer's total payments of class 1 national insurance are £45,000 or less he can recover 103 per cent of the SMP paid.

The extra amount is to compensate him for the employer's national insurance payable on the SMP.

If the employer's total class 1 national insurance payments are more than £45,000 per year, the employer can recover 92% of the SMP paid.

Employer vs Employee

With salary sacrifice pensions the idea is that neither the employee nor the employer is worse off.

However, when it comes to the payment of non-cash benefits during maternity leave, it is possible the employer will be left out of pocket.

This is because employers have to continue providing any non-cash benefits that have been agreed under the contract of employment for up to 52 weeks (i.e. the full period of maternity leave).

Non-cash benefits include things like company cars and childcare vouchers.

There is some debate as to whether employer pension contributions have to be paid for the full 52 weeks of maternity leave but most accept that they have to be paid for the entire 39 week period of paid maternity leave.

The full amount has to be paid as though the woman was working normally and had taken no maternity leave at all.

Clearly paying pension contributions could be more expensive to the employer than paying statutory maternity pay.

Maternity Allowance

Maternity allowance is paid to women who are employed but not entitled to SMP. Maternity allowance is based on your earnings, so a salary sacrifice arrangement may reduce your entitlement to maternity allowance.

Chapter 11

How to Implement Salary Sacrifice Arrangements

It is important to point out that salary sacrifice must be a *contractual agreement*, not an informal arrangement between you and your employer.

In other words, you have to change your employment contract and this has to be done in writing.

Your contract of employment can be altered by using a simple agreement letter, signed by both you and your employer, and many pension companies provide sample documentation. This letter should be kept with your employment contract.

The new agreement must state what benefit is being received in exchange for the sacrificed salary.

Salary sacrifice can start at any time during the year but it's important that the potential future salary is given up before it is treated as received for tax and national insurance purposes. Your terms of employment must be changed *before* the salary sacrifice commences and the sacrificed amount should appear on your payslip as a salary reduction, rather than a deduction.

HMRC is not against salary sacrifice but could challenge the arrangement if it has not been set up correctly and the paperwork is not in order.

For example, the arrangement could be challenged if the employee can revert to the original pay package at any time.

However, it is important to point out that, once you opt for a salary sacrifice pension, you do not have to stick with your decision forever. Most well-structured salary sacrifice arrangements have an annual renewal date which allows you to opt out.

According to Scottish Life, a contract alteration will usually last for 12 months so that it fits in with salary reviews: "The salary exchange agreement should state that the variation is time bounded and that the original contract will be reinstated at the end of the salary exchange period. A new agreement should therefore be arranged at the end of each agreement period if the salary exchange is to continue."

Generally speaking a salary sacrifice arrangement should not last for less than 12 months. However, the agreement can be cancelled if you experience a 'lifestyle event' such as divorce, marriage, pregnancy or a partner's redundancy.

Getting HMRC Approval

HM Revenue & Customs does not have to be notified of salary sacrifice arrangements. However, after the arrangement is set up employers can ask their local tax offices to confirm that the correct tax treatment is being applied.

HMRC will probably want to see evidence that the employment contracts have been changed correctly and payslips before and after the sacrifice.

Details can also be sent to:

HMRC Clearances Team
Alexander House
21 Victoria Avenue
Southend-on-Sea
SS99 1BD

This gives the employer reassurance the arrangement has been implemented correctly.

Payslips and P60s

Strictly speaking your new post salary sacrifice payslip should not show your old salary, with the sacrificed amount shown as a deduction.

However, HMRC's guidance notes state that if the employment contract has been changed correctly, the payslip is less important.

However, if there are issues surrounding the employment contract, the payslip may be used to determine whether the salary sacrifice is valid.

HMRC recognises that some payroll software can only store one value for the employee's salary. This could create problems when calculating overtime and other benefits based on the higher pre-sacrifice reference salary.

However, as long as the contract has been modified correctly, and makes it clear that the employee is entitled to a reduced salary and specified benefits, HMRC should not invalidate the salary sacrifice.

HMRC's guidance notes point out that non-taxable benefits-in-kind must not be carried forward to the P60.

Finally, I would strongly recommend speaking to a financial advisor who has experience of salary sacrifice pensions before diving in and setting one up yourself.

Chapter 12

Sacrificing Bonuses

You can also sacrifice a bonus and have an equivalent amount paid into your pension plan by your employer.

The treatment of discretionary and contractual bonuses is different.

Discretionary Bonuses

No written agreement is needed if the bonus is discretionary. If the bonus is not part of your existing contract of employment then no change to that contract is required to sacrifice it – you can simply request your employer to pay the amount into your pension plan and no paperwork is needed.

Having said that the bonus may have to be sacrificed before the employee becomes entitled to it.

Contractual Bonuses

Contractual bonuses have to be treated in the same way as a regular salary sacrifice – an agreement to sacrifice the bonus must be in place before the bonus is received.

According to Aegon, a contractual bonus can be sacrificed at any point until it becomes a Schedule E emolument: "For a non-director this is the date the employee receives it. For a director establishing the date is more difficult. For example it could be the date when the bonus is signed off in the accounts and approved by shareholders."

Example – Bonus Sacrifice

An employee, who is not a director, is contractually entitled to a bonus each year, based on the company's profits

↓

The company's year end is 31 January

↓

The company's accounts are ready on 31 July, allowing the bonus to be calculated

↓

Payment of the bonus is on 31 October

↓

The employee is informed in writing on 31st August that the bonus will be £10,000 and given the option to sacrifice the bonus in return for a £10,000 employer pension contribution

↓

The employee chooses to sacrifice the bonus and returns the completed documentation to the company by 30 September

↓

The completed documentation makes it clear that the employee has given up his contractual right to the bonus and does not have the right to change his mind

↓

This should be a successful sacrifice because it was given up before it would have been treated as received on 31 October

If the employee in the above example is a higher-rate taxpayer, he or she would have ended up with an after-tax cash bonus of just £5,800 (£10,000 less 40% tax less 2% national insurance).

By opting for an employer pension contribution the employee ends up with a pension investment of up to £11,380 (£10,000 plus 13.8% employer's national insurance).

Legal advice may be necessary to decide if a bonus is contractual or discretionary.

Chapter 13

How to Protect Your Child Benefit

Child benefit is an extremely valuable benefit worth £1,056 for the first child and £697 per year for each subsequent child.

So a couple with two children will receive £1,753 per year tax free.

You can keep receiving child benefit until your children are 16 years of age or until age 20 if they are enrolled in 'relevant education' (the likes of GCSEs, A Levels, and NVQs to level 3, but not degree courses).

That's the good news. The bad news, as we now know, is that the Government has proposed taking away child benefit from all higher-rate taxpayers from January 2013.

For the current 2011/12 tax year, a higher-rate taxpayer is someone who earns more than £42,475. The same income level applies for the 2012/13 tax year.

The proposed change to child benefit is an all or nothing measure and therefore extremely unfair. For example, if your taxable income goes up by just £1 and this takes you over the threshold into higher rate tax, you will lose your entire child benefit entitlement.

In other words, an extra £1 of income will cost you £1,753 if you have two children.

The measure is also unfair because a family with only one earner on £44,000 will lose all of its child benefit. However, a family with two people earning, say, £40,000 each (£80,000 in total), will not lose any benefit.

Protecting Child Benefit with Salary Sacrifice

If the proposal to withdraw child benefit from higher-rate taxpayers becomes law, a salary sacrifice pension could provide a useful way to reduce the financial sting.

Of course, a lot could happen between now and 2013. If there is significant political opposition to the proposal, the measure may be watered down in some way.

Furthermore, anti-avoidance measures could be introduced to prevent taxpayers from reducing their taxable incomes below the higher-rate threshold. Nevertheless, it's interesting to see how much money could potentially be saved with a salary sacrifice arrangement, in the absence of any anti-avoidance measures.

Example

Cheryl has two children under 16 years of age, earns a salary of £45,000 and personally contributes £4,000 per year to a pension plan. The taxman tops up her pension contribution with an extra £1,000, bringing her total contribution to £5,000.

Because she is a higher-rate taxpayer she will lose her entire child benefit payment, currently £1,753 per year.

Cheryl decides to stop making pension contributions herself and asks her employer to make them on her behalf.

She sacrifices £5,000 of salary to compensate her employer and, as a result, becomes a basic-rate taxpayer. This means she will keep receiving child benefit.

In total she ends up with £2,101 more disposable income per year and her pension contributions are increased by £690 per year. All in all, she is better off to the tune of £2,791 per year.

This example is based on the current year's income tax and national insurance rates. However, it clearly illustrates how powerful a salary sacrifice pension arrangement could be at protecting your child benefit payments from 2013.

Cheryl's Take Home Pay Increases By £2,101

	Before Salary Sacrifice	After Salary Sacrifice
	£	£
Salary	45,000	40,000
Less:		
Income tax	7,505 *	6,505
National insurance	4,281	3,933
Pension contribution	4,000	0
Plus:		
Child benefit	0	1,753
Disposable income	**29,214**	**31,315**

... And Her Pension Pot Increases By £690

	Before Salary Sacrifice	After Salary Sacrifice
	£	£
Employee contribution	4,000	-
Taxman's top up	1,000	-
Employer contribution	-	5,000
Employer's NI saving	-	690
Total	**5,000**	**5,690**

* Reduced by £505 higher-rate income tax relief (her tax relief is restricted to the amount of earnings taxed at 40%).

Chapter 14

Future Changes to National Insurance

In the March 2011 Budget the Government announced that it will consult on reforms to integrate the operation of income tax and national insurance.

This announcement seems to recognise that national insurance is just tax by another name. It would be far more honest to have a basic rate of income tax of 32%, instead of 20% income tax plus 12% national insurance.

A merger of income tax and national insurance would remove the need to set up a salary sacrifice arrangement to reclaim all the tax on your pension contributions. Employees would be able to obtain full tax relief by making their pension contributions personally.

However, don't expect this change to take place any time soon. The Chancellor in his Budget speech stated that:

"This huge task will therefore require a great deal of consultation and take a number of years to complete, but it is time we took this historic step to simplify dramatically our tax system and make it fit for the modern age."

Personally, I am sceptical as to whether such a radical reform of the tax system will take place, at least not before the next general election in May 2015.

There would be winners but also losers and the coalition Government will probably not be able to afford creating more losers, following years of public spending cuts.

Writing in *The Times* former Chancellor of the Exchequer Nigel Lawson, who investigated such a reform in the 1980s, has warned George Osborne that merging the two taxes is a "huge elephant trap":

"A merger of the two would, in practice, be very costly and (because there would be both winners and losers) highly unpopular, all to little advantage.

"So I say to George: 'Don't go there'. In fact, I suspect he is already backtracking. His Budget speech was reassuringly careful, ruling out the application of national insurance contributions (unlike income tax) to pensions or savings income and (although describing it as a 'historic step') seeming to commit himself to little more than tidying up administration of the two systems, which may be very sensible but is scarcely 'historic'."

Whether such a significant change to the tax system is practicable, remains to be seen. However, there is little doubt that a Conservative Government would be committed to such a change on ideological grounds.

Such a change would make taxpayers more aware of the fact that they are actually paying 32% tax (plus an additional 13.8% tax paid by the employer), making it potentially less difficult to encourage support for a smaller role for Government in the economy and lower tax rates.

Appendix 1

Sample Employment Letter

1 May 2011

Dear John,

With effect from 1 June 2011 your salary will be reduced from £30,000 per annum to £28,529 per annum for a period of 12 months.

In return the company will make a contribution of £1,471 into your pension scheme. A contribution of £203 will also be made representing our national insurance saving.

By signing this letter you are confirming your agreement.

Yours sincerely,

For XYZ Ltd   Date ....

I agree that my salary should be contractually reduced as described above.

Signed ....

Date ....

Note: This letter contains sample wording for illustrative purposes. You should obtain your own legal advice.

Appendix 2

Useful Links

The following links on the HMRC website may be useful:

www.hmrc.gov.uk/specialist/salary_sacrifice.htm

www.hmrc.gov.uk/specialist/salary_sacrifice.pdf

www.hmrc.gov.uk/specialist/sal-sac-question-and-answers.htm

www.hmrc.gov.uk/manuals/eimanual/eim42750.htm

www.hmrc.gov.uk/manuals/eimanual/eim42774.htm

www.hmrc.gov.uk/employers/sml-salary-sacrifice.pdf

Lightning Source UK Ltd.
Milton Keynes UK

177285UK00003B/13/P